The Life of
Susan B. Anthony

By Kathleen Connors

Gareth Stevens
Publishing

Please visit our website, www.garethstevens.com. For a free color catalog of all our high-quality books, call toll free 1-800-542-2595 or fax 1-877-542-2596.

Library of Congress Cataloging-in-Publication Data

Connors, Kathleen.
Susan B. Anthony / by Kathleen Connors.
  p. cm. — (Famous lives)
Includes index.
ISBN 978-1-4824-0428-9 (pbk.)
ISBN 978-1-4824-0429-6 (6-pack)
ISBN 978-1-4824-0425-8 (library binding)
1. Anthony, Susan B. — (Susan Brownell), — 1820-1906 — Juvenile literature. 2. Feminists — United States — Biography — Juvenile literature. 3. Suffragists — United States — Biography — Juvenile literature. I. Connors, Kathleen. II. Title.
HQ1413.A55 C66 2014
305.42—dc23

First Edition

Published in 2014 by
Gareth Stevens Publishing
111 East 14th Street, Suite 349
New York, NY 10003

Designer: Nicholas Domiano
Editor: Kristen Rajczak

Photo credits: Cover, pp. 1, 21 Photo Inc/Photo Researchers/Getty Images; p. 5 Scewing/Wikimedia Commons; p. 7 John Howe Kent/George Eastman House/Getty Images; p. 9 PhotoQuest/Archive Photos/Getty Images; p. 11 Library of Congress/Wikimedia Commons; p. 13 Fotosearch/Archive Photos/Getty Images; p. 15 Mu/Wikimedia Commons; p. 17 Yaksar/Wikimedia Commons; p. 19 Kean Collection/Archive Photos/Getty Images.

Printed in the United States of America

CPSIA compliance information: Batch #CW14GS: For further information contact Gareth Stevens, New York, New York at 1-800-542-2595.

Contents

Boldface words appear in the glossary.

Her Key Role

Susan B. Anthony was a strong voice in support of **civil rights** for all. She spent her life fighting for women's **suffrage**. Today, she's remembered as an important part of the cause's success.

5

For Equality Early

Susan was born in 1820 in Massachusetts. Her family moved to Battenville, New York, when she was a child. There, they became part of the antislavery movement. A group of **abolitionists** met at their home.

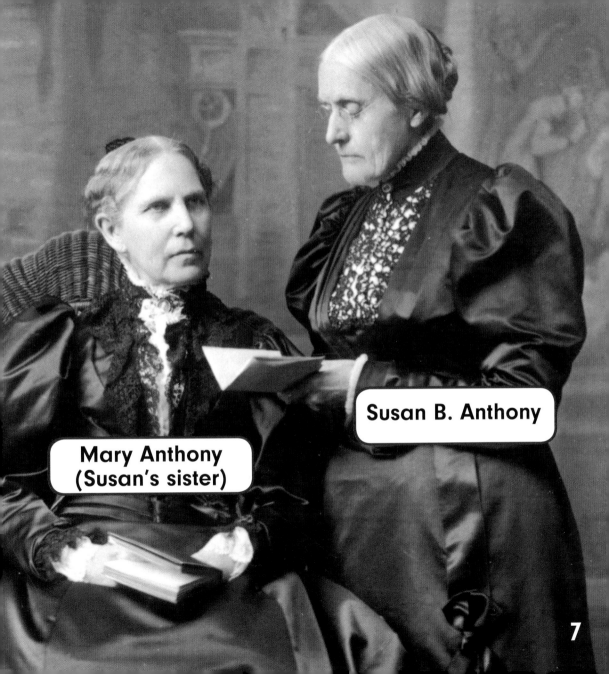

Mary Anthony
(Susan's sister)

Susan B. Anthony

Susan was teaching in the late 1840s when she began to notice women's inequality. She found out that teachers who were men were paid $10 each month, while the women were paid only $2.50! Susan thought that was unfair.

An Important Friend

In 1851, Susan met Elizabeth Cady Stanton. Elizabeth was in favor of women's suffrage. She had helped plan the Seneca Falls Convention, a big meeting about the cause. With her new friend's support, Susan joined the movement.

Susan B. Anthony

Elizabeth Cady Stanton

11

Spreading the Message

Susan began speaking out about women's property, or land, rights. She also believed women should have more equality in marriage. At the time, only men could own property and make decisions for their families.

Not everyone agreed with Susan about women's rights. They threw things at her during speeches and even **threatened** to hurt her! But Susan continued to spread the word by speaking, hanging posters, and giving out booklets.

Susan and Elizabeth formed the National Woman Suffrage Association in 1869. They wanted an **amendment** to the US **Constitution** giving women the right to vote. It was first presented to Congress in 1878.

A PETITION

FOR

UNIVERSAL SUFFRAGE.

To the Senate and House of Representatives:

The undersigned, Women of the United States, respectfully ask an amendment of the Constitution that shall prohibit the several States from disfranchising any of their citizens on the ground of sex.

In making our demand for Suffrage, we would call your attention to the fact that we represent fifteen million people—one half the entire population of the country—intelligent, virtuous, native-born American citizens; and yet stand outside the pale of political recognition.

The Constitution classes us as "free people," and counts us *whole* persons in the basis of representation; and yet are we governed without our consent, compelled to pay taxes without appeal, and punished for violations of law without choice of judge or juror.

The experience of all ages, the Declarations of the Fathers, the Statute Laws of our own day, and the fearful revolution through which we have just passed, all prove the uncertain tenure of life, liberty and property so long as the ballot—the only weapon of self-protection—is not in the hand of every citizen.

Therefore, as you are now amending the Constitution, and, in harmony with advancing civilization, placing new safeguards round the individual rights of four millions of emancipated slaves, we ask that you extend the right of Suffrage to Woman—the only remaining class of disfranchised citizens—and thus fulfil your Constitutional obligation "to Guarantee to every State in the Union a Republican form of Government."

As all partial application of Republican principles must ever breed a complicated legislation as well as a discontented people, we would pray your Honorable Body, in order to simplify the machinery of government and ensure domestic tranquillity, that you legislate hereafter for persons, citizens, tax-payers, and not for class or caste.

For justice and equality your petitioners will ever pray.

NAMES.	RESIDENCE.
Elizabeth Cady Stanton	New York
Susan B. Anthony	Rochester — N.Y.
Antoinette Brown Blackwell	New York
Lucy Stone	Newark N. Jersey
Joanna S. Morse	48 Livingston Brooklyn
Ernestine L. Rose	New York
Harriet E. Eaton	6 West 14th Street N.Y.
Catharine C. Wilkeson	83 Clinton Place New York
Elizabeth R. Tilton	48 Livingston St. Brooklyn
Mary Fowler Gilbert	295 W. 19th St New York
Mary E. Gilbert	New York
M. Griffith	New York

Voting Power

In 1872, Susan took her support for women's suffrage even further. She and some other women voted for president! Susan was **arrested** and fined, but she refused to pay. In the following years, her beliefs remained strong.

19

Susan died in 1906, years before the Nineteenth Amendment passed in 1920. It gave women the right to vote! In her honor, the amendment was called the Susan B. Anthony Amendment.

Timeline

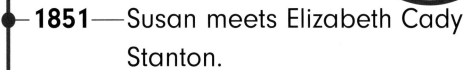

- **1820**——Susan is born.
- **1851**——Susan meets Elizabeth Cady Stanton.
- **1869**——Susan and Elizabeth form the National Woman Suffrage Association.
- **1872**——Susan votes and is arrested for it.
- **1906**——Susan dies.
- **1920**——The Nineteenth Amendment gives women the right to vote.

Glossary

abolitionist: one who fights to end slavery

amendment: a change or addition to a constitution

arrest: to take charge of someone by law

civil rights: the freedoms granted to us by law

constitution: the basic laws by which a country or state is governed

suffrage: the right of voting

threaten: to state possible actions that would cause harm

For More Information

Books

Malaspina, Ann. *Heart on Fire: Susan B. Anthony Votes for President*. Chicago, IL: Albert Whitman & Co., 2012.

Murphy, Claire Rudolf. *Marching with Aunt Susan: Susan B. Anthony and the Fight for Women's Suffrage*. Atlanta, GA: Peachtree, 2011.

Websites

National Susan B. Anthony Museum & House

susanbanthonyhouse.org

Read more about Susan B. Anthony's life, and plan a visit to the museum dedicated to her.

Women's Suffrage

teacher.scholastic.com/activities/suffrage/

Find out how women earned the right to vote and much more on Scholastic's website.

Publisher's note to educators and parents: Our editors have carefully reviewed these websites to ensure that they are suitable for students. Many websites change frequently, however, and we cannot guarantee that a site's future contents will continue to meet our high standards of quality and educational value. Be advised that students should be closely supervised whenever they access the Internet.

Index